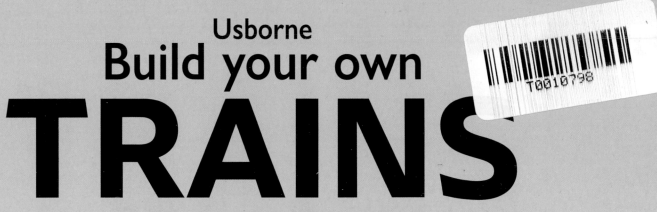

Usborne
Build your own
TRAINS
Sticker Book

Illustrated by Adrian Mann

Designed by Marc Maynard
Written by Simon Tudhope

Consultant: Andy Coates

Contents

steam train

This train sounded like a mighty animal panting down the tracks. Powered by the huge boiler in front of the engineer, it used high-pressure steam to drive its wheels.

STATISTICS

Active: 1924 – 1964
Top speed: 65mph
Length: 72ft
Weight: 77 tons
Horsepower: 1,600hp

STATISTICS

Active: 2012 – present

Top speed: 224mph

Length: 75ft

Weight: 44 tons

Horsepower: 16,300hp

High speed train

One of the fastest trains on the planet. Fields and trees flash past as it surges between major cities at over 200mph.

Switch engine

This stocky machine moves cars around railroad yards. Built for huge power at low speeds, it can handle freight twenty times its own weight.

Electric train

Running on busy routes between towns and cities, this train draws all its power from overhead lines. It's fast, quiet and completely smoke-free.

STATISTICS

Active: 2010 – present
Top speed: 100mph
Length: 75ft, 6in
Weight: 50 tons
Horsepower: 2,100hp

Cog locomotive

With its cog wheels gripping the track, this curious machine climbs steep mountain slopes. As it huffs and puffs towards the summit, the boiler's kept flat so it won't overheat.

STATISTICS

Active: 1908 – present
Top speed: 5mph
Length: 16ft, 5in
Weight: 13.2 tons
Horsepower: 600hp

Tram

This vehicle glides around town along tracks in the road. Drawing its power from overhead lines, it's the smoothest way to travel through the busy streets.

Freight train

Clattering across the lonely plains, wheels screeching as it goes around the bends, this train is over one hundred cars long and packed with heavy freight.

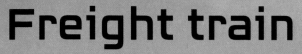

STATISTICS

Active: 1972 – present

Top speed: 65mph

Length: 59ft

Weight: 125 tons

Horsepower: 4,000hp

Funicular

These little cars run on separate tracks but work together to climb steep mountain slopes. They're connected by a steel cable, and as one car moves down the slope, it pulls the other car up.

STATISTICS

Active: 2001 – present
Top speed: 22mph
Length: 34ft, 5in
Weight: 17 tons
Horsepower: 680hp

Monorail

This train glides around the city on a single rail. The passengers sit back and enjoy the view as it cruises above the busy streets.

Monorail

Connecting the city

STATISTICS

Active: 1988 – present

Top speed: 20mph

Length: 18ft, 5in

Weight: 3.9 tons

Horsepower: 300hp

Diesel-electric train

Using a huge diesel engine to generate its own electricity, this train can run anywhere from bustling cities to sleepy country lines.

STATISTICS

Active: 1975 – present

Top speed: 148mph

Length: 58ft, 5in

Weight: 77 tons

Horsepower: 2,250hp

Underground train

Here's the train that keeps big cities on the move. Clattering through a network of dark tunnels and brightly-lit stations, it carries thousands of people to work each day.

STATISTICS

Active: 2010 – present

Top speed: 62mph

Length: 57ft

Weight: 38 tons

Horsepower: 2,250hp

Rocket

This is where train travel really began. *Rocket* won a competition to run the world's first steam passenger service. With its engine generating the same power as twenty horses, it blasted transportation into the modern age.

STATISTICS

Active: 1830 – 1840

Top speed: 30mph

Length: 12ft

Weight: 4.7 tons

Horsepower: 20hp

Mallard

The fastest steam locomotive ever built. With its enormous wheels spinning around almost nine times every second, *Mallard* pushed steam power to its limits.

STATISTICS

Active: 1938 – 1963
Top speed: 126mph
Length: 70ft
Weight: 115.3 tons
Horsepower: 1,800hp

Orient Express

It's 1933 and this luxury train is steaming across Europe, from Paris to Istanbul. In the evening, the seats in its oak-panelled compartments are turned into beds, and the restaurant serves fine food and champagne.

STATISTICS

Active: 1915 – 1970
Top speed: 65mph
Length: 55ft
Weight: 108 tons
Horsepower: 1,400hp

Trans-Siberian

Rumbling through 9,000 miles of Russian wilderness, this train is making its way from Moscow to Vladivostok. It takes six days to reach its destination and runs on the longest railroad line in the world.

STATISTICS

Active: 1965 – present

Top speed: 62mph

Length: 57ft, 9in

Weight: 128 tons

Horsepower: 3,948hp

Channel Tunnel

This high speed train glides under the sea, through a tunnel that connects England to France. You can board in London at 10am and be in Paris in time for lunch.

STATISTICS

Active: 1994 – present
Top speed: 186mph
Length: 72ft, 10in
Weight: 75.5 tons
Horsepower: 16,400hp

Flying Scotsman

Charging across the rolling fields, over the hills and bridges, this train ran 400 miles from London to Edinburgh without stopping once on the way.

STATISTICS

Active: 1928 – 1936
Top speed: 100mph
Length: 70ft
Weight: 108 tons
Horsepower: 1,400hp

The Ghan

Running right through the heart of Australia, past snapping crocodiles and scorching deserts, this train travels from Darwin on the north coast to Adelaide on the south.

STATISTICS

Active: 1996 – present
Top speed: 71mph
Length: 72ft
Weight: 146 tons
Horsepower: 4,020hp

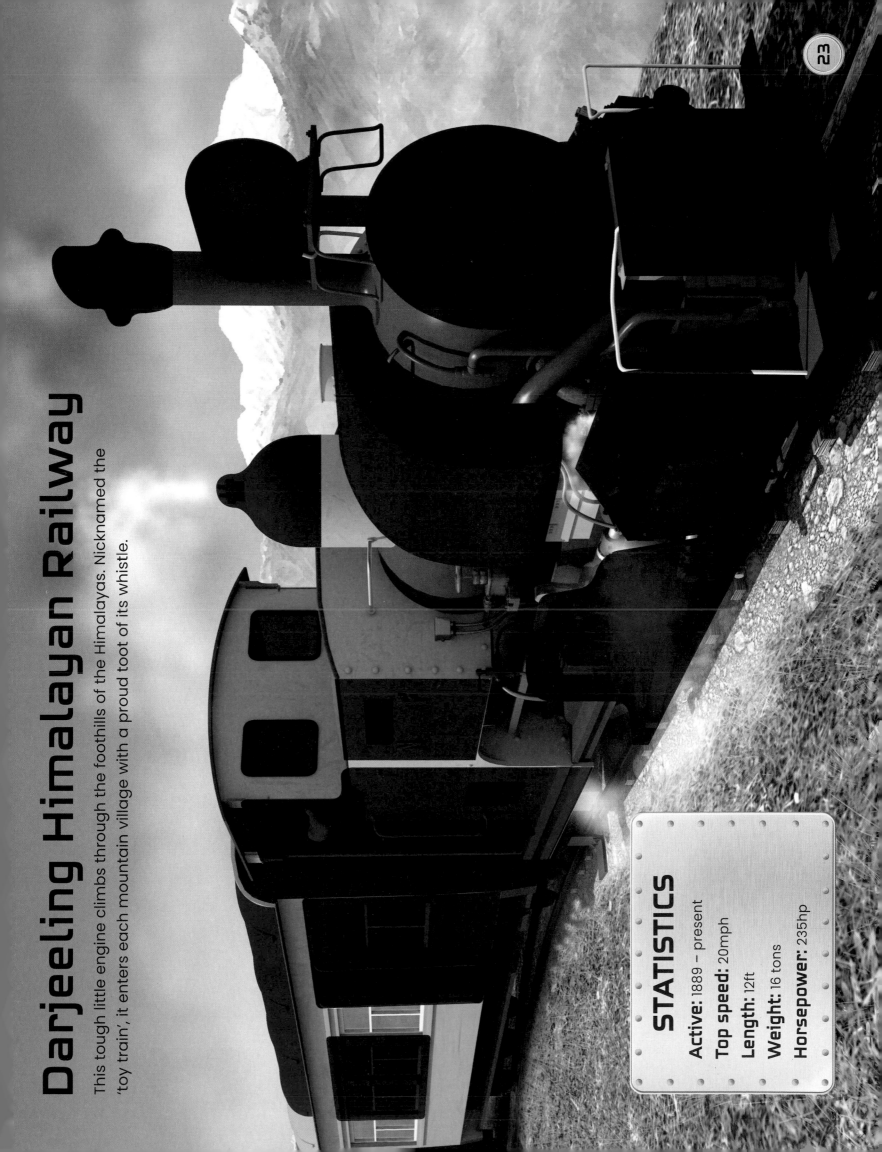

Darjeeling Himalayan Railway

This tough little engine climbs through the foothills of the Himalayas. Nicknamed the 'toy train', it enters each mountain village with a proud toot of its whistle.

STATISTICS

Active: 1889 – present

Top speed: 20mph

Length: 12ft

Weight: 16 tons

Horsepower: 235hp

Glossary

- **BOILER:** a big barrel on a steam locomotive that's in front of the cab. It contains water and steam at high pressure.

- **CAB:** a compartment in a locomotive where the engineer works

- **DIESEL ENGINE:** an engine that uses a type of fuel called diesel to generate its power

- **ELECTRIC ENGINE:** an engine that uses electricity to generate its power

- **FREIGHT:** cargo that's transported in large quantities

- **HORSEPOWER:** the power an engine can produce per second. The number in the statistics box is the maximum power that engine can produce.

- **LOCOMOTIVE:** the vehicle on a train that provides the power. This is where the engineer works, and is usually at the front of the train.

- **OVERHEAD LINES:** wires above a railroad track that carry electricity

- **STREAMLINED:** an object that has been shaped to move through the air as quickly as possible

- **TRAIN:** a locomotive with cars or wagons attached

Note on the statistics boxes: The 'Length' and 'Weight' measurements are for the front vehicle of each train.

Digital manipulation by Keith Furnival

Edited by Sam Taplin and Phil Clarke

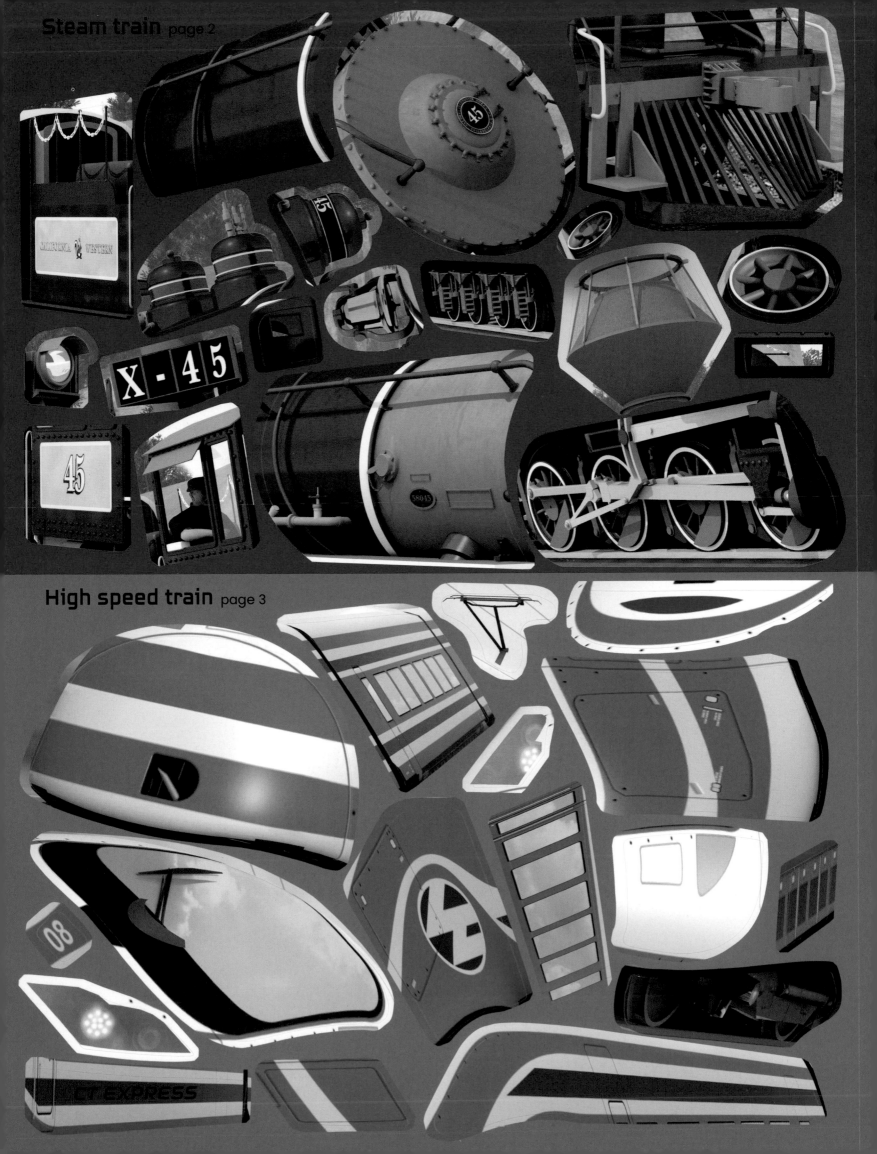

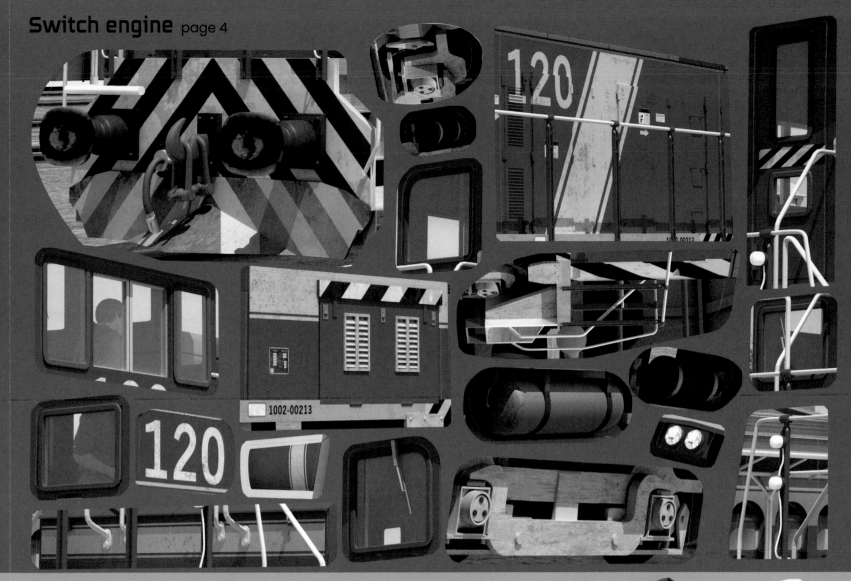

Cog MOUNTAIN Railway

2

OLD BETSY

102

WESTON PIER

MAIN STREET TRAM CO.

WESTON PIER

102

Funicular page 10

Monorail page 11

CITY

Monorail

Connecting the city

Diesel-electric train page 12

43058

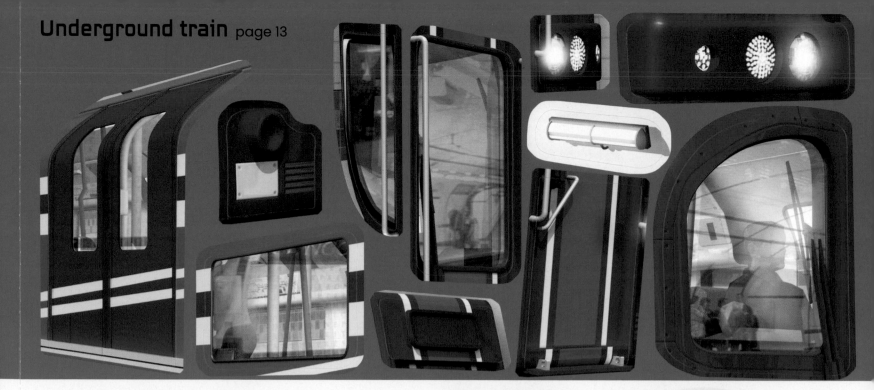

Rocket pages 14-15

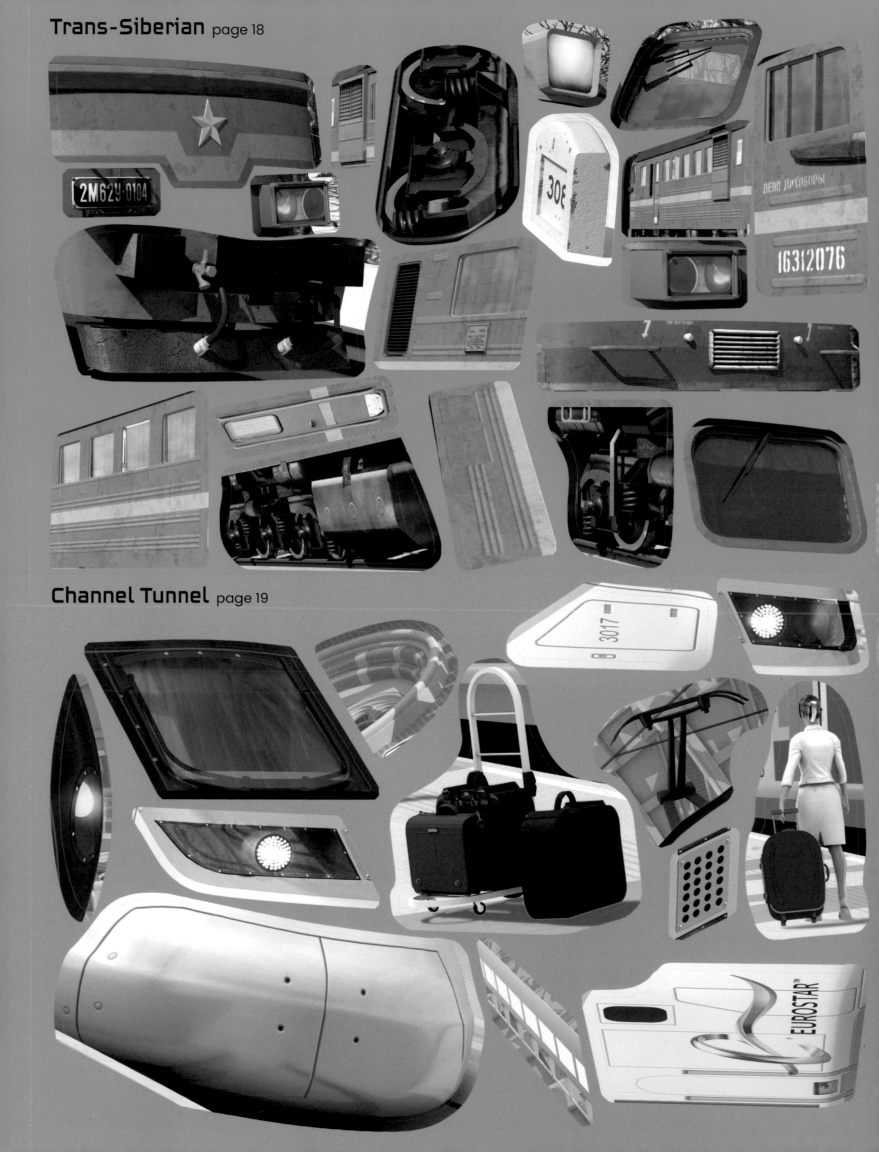

Channel Tunnel page 19

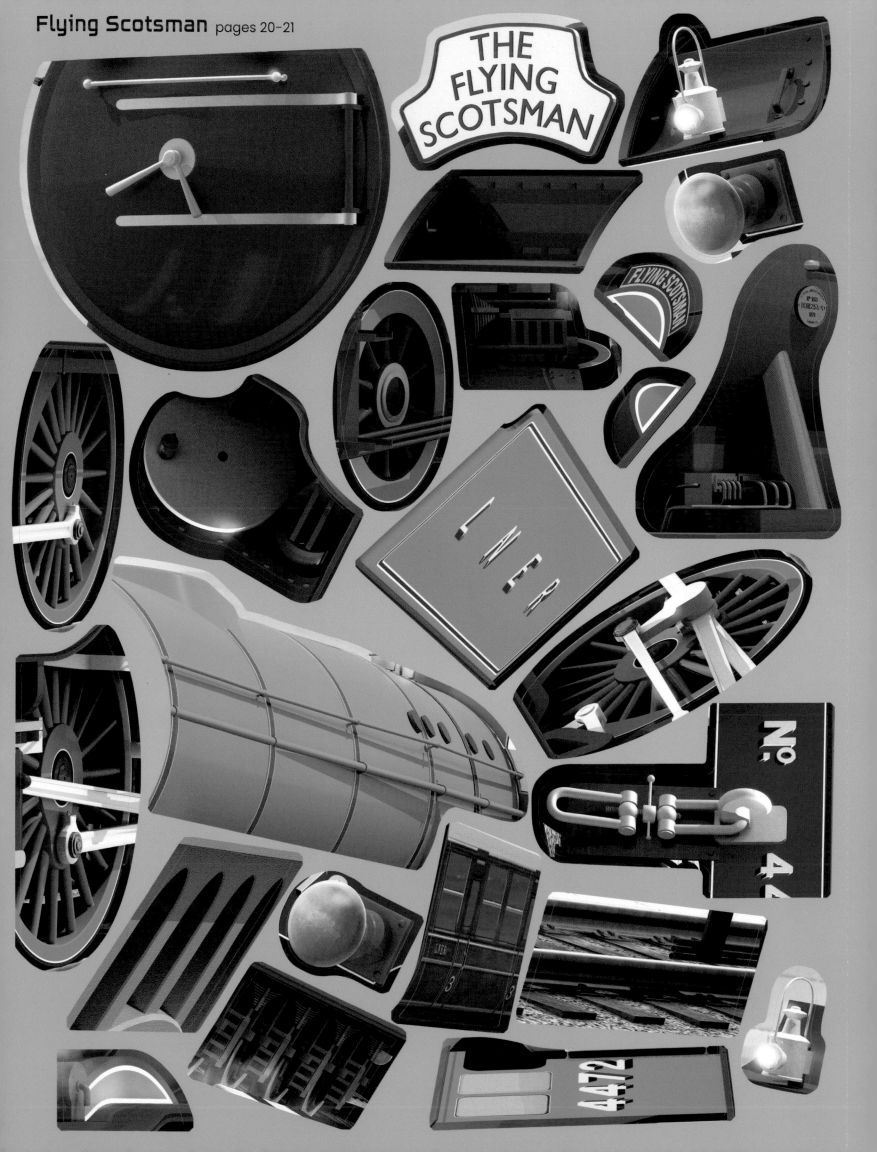